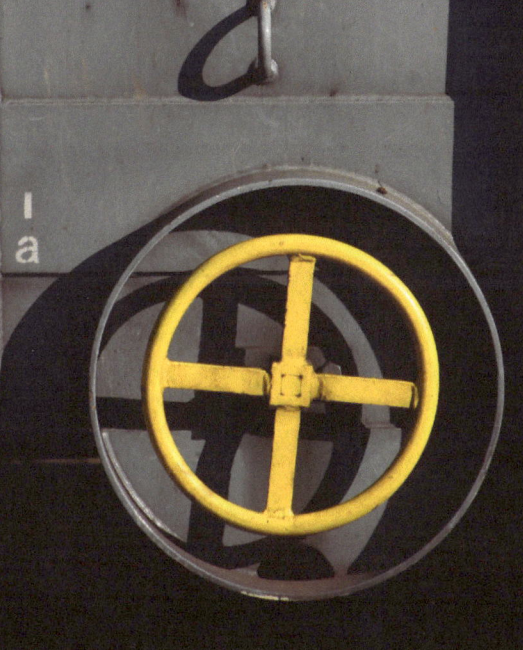

A Mark Dahle Portfolio

Return Trip

Present Divestment #2

Mark Dahle Portfolios can be read in a few minutes and enjoyed for a lifetime.

This portfolio includes the second story in the Present Divestment series, a photo of a beautiful 36 x 24 inch painting (at the right) and twenty-five outstanding photographs from Basel, Switzerland.

Unlike many picture books, the text is unrelated to the paintings and photographs. This might seem weird at first. One thing that helps is to order more portfolios until you get used to it. Space is provided for you to create your own pictures of the return trip if you like.

Photographs in this book are available in limited editions. See http://www.MarkDahle.com for more information and for previews of upcoming portfolios.

We do our best to create portfolios free of editing mistakes. But it's hard to catch everything. We reward people who report errors in any Mark Dahle portfolio. For details see MarkDahle.com/Typos.html or send an email to MarkDahle@aol.com with the subject line "Typos." Thanks!

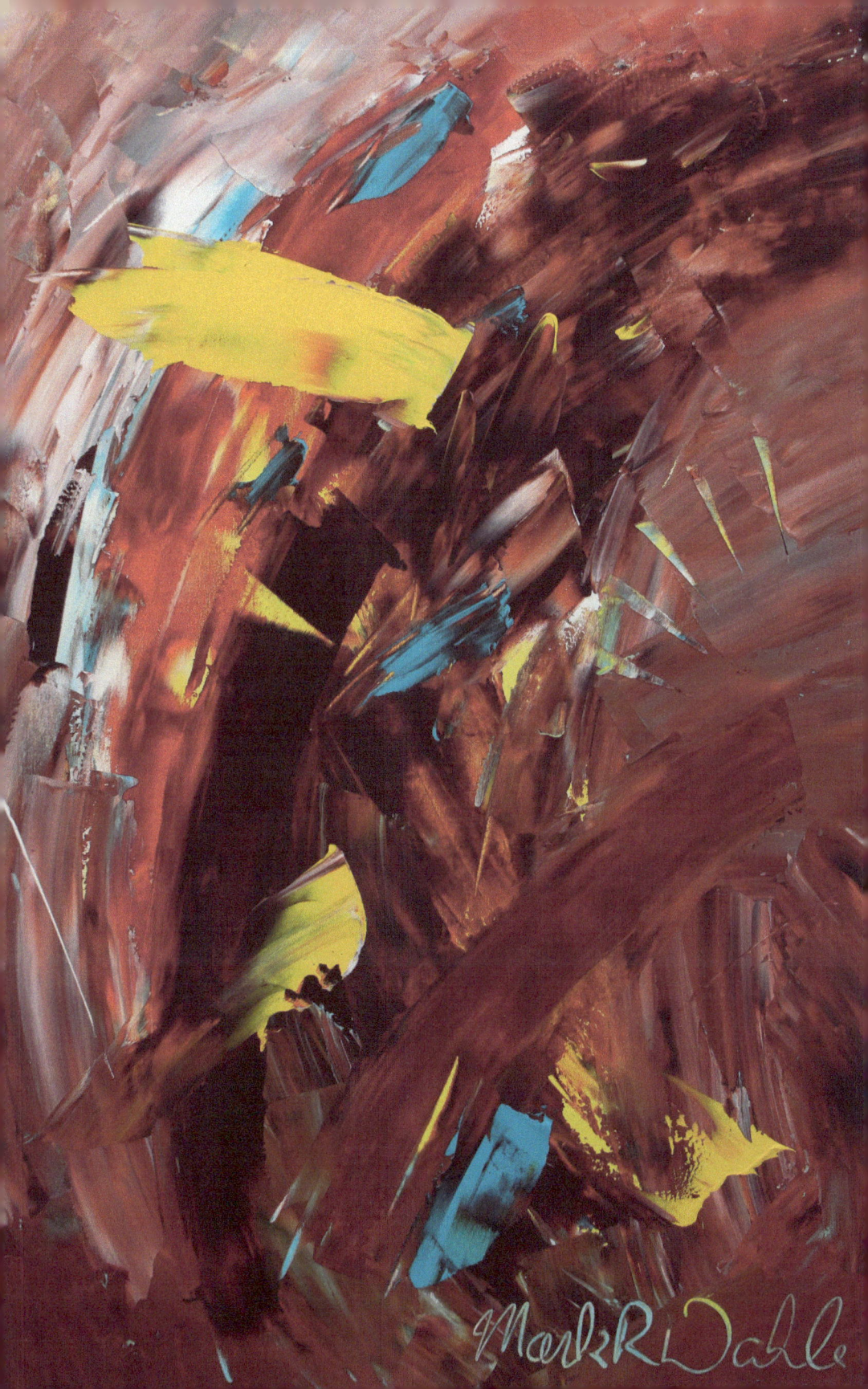

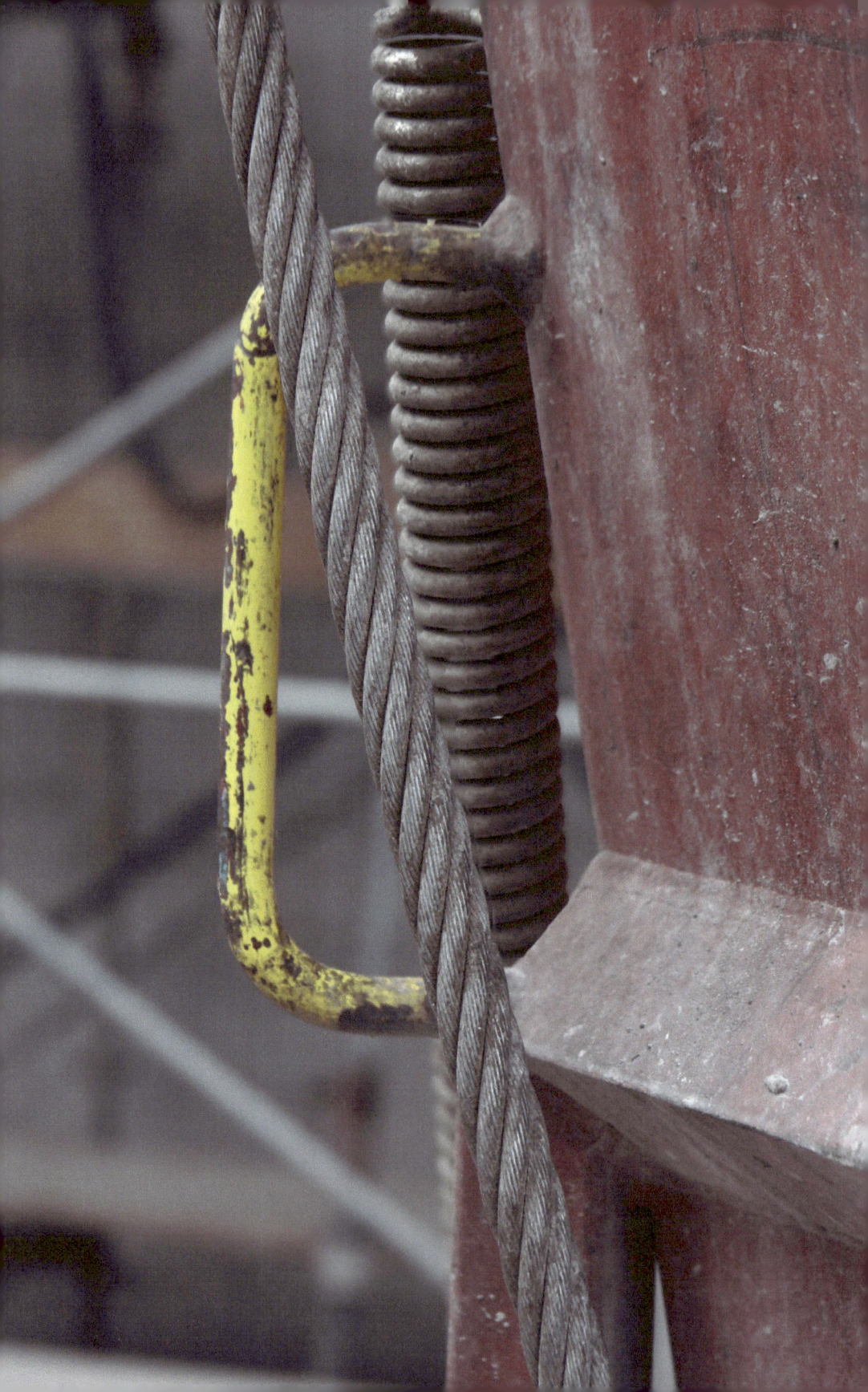

"This is the second timeshift he's missed. I can't believe he's not here."

"It's a first, alright."

"J-rex obsesses over *everything*. I couldn't believe it when he missed the launch. But missing the return? How could he not be here for the return?"

Lat looked up from the controls and glanced at Se and Paul. "He said it was unavoidable."

"Right. Unavoidable. The first time we try hyptrolysis with Jon? What could possibly be more important than being here? If this works, it'll be the first time Jon has gone outside the perimeter. He could have found *anything*."

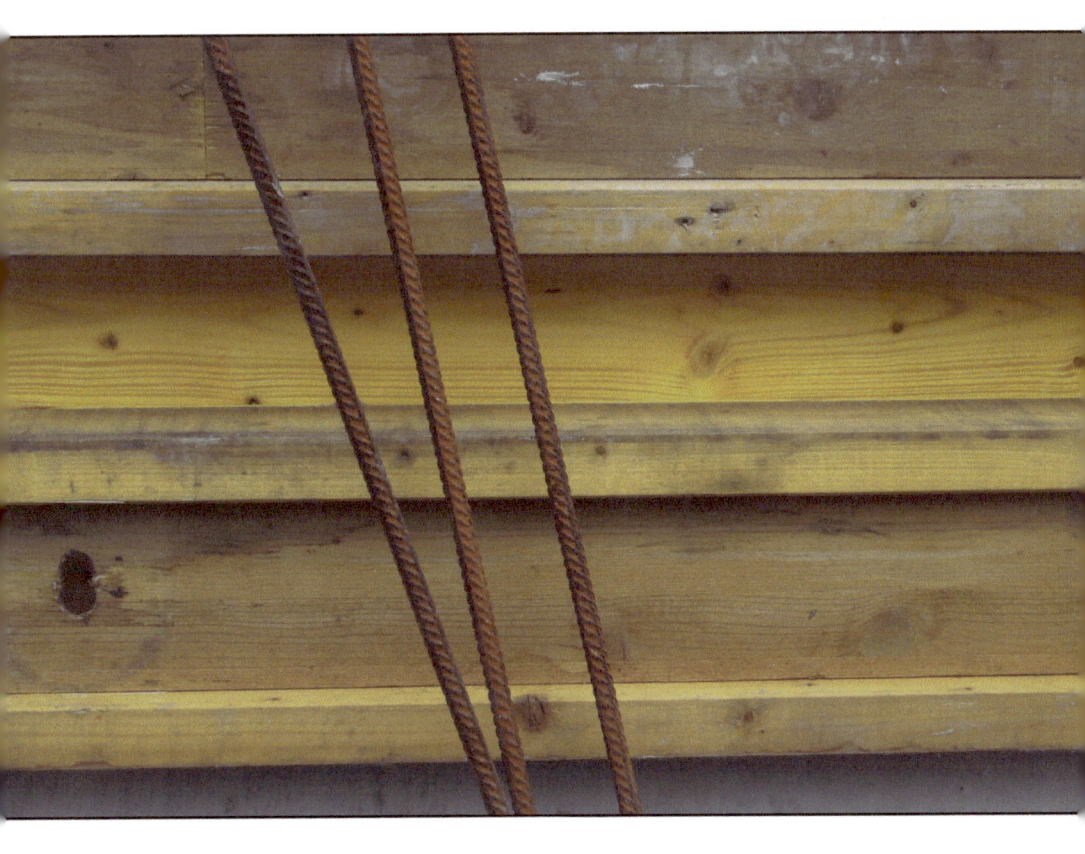

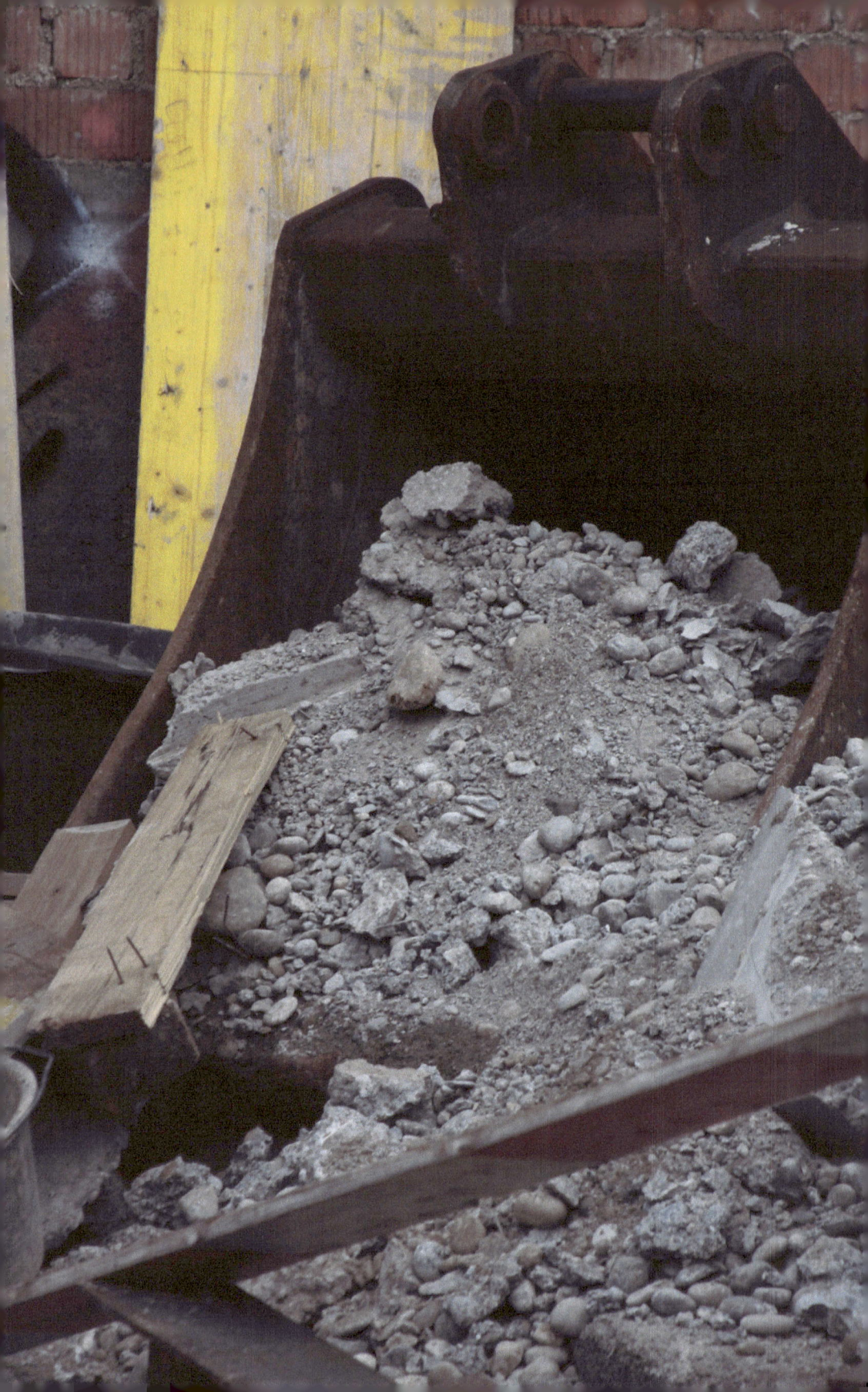

Lat didn't glance up this time. "He might not return, you know."

"Don't say that."

"The perimeter is fairly safe – as safe as they can make it. But hyptrolysis instructed him to go beyond the perimeter. Who knows what he found – or what condition he'll be in when he returns. *If* he makes it back."

"Is that why the extra MediCorp team showed up?"

"The last thing J-rex did before he left was to order that extra Med team to be in place, just in case."

"Do you think he's watching?"

"J-rex is *always* watching. You don't have to worry about that."

Lat didn't say all he was thinking – partly because he was certain that J-rex *was* watching. The only question was: Where was he watching *from*? Who was he with? What was he doing that was so important that he couldn't be with the team?

Lat had a suspicion, but he didn't like to think it, and he wasn't about to say it out loud: J-rex wasn't present because this time it was too dangerous.

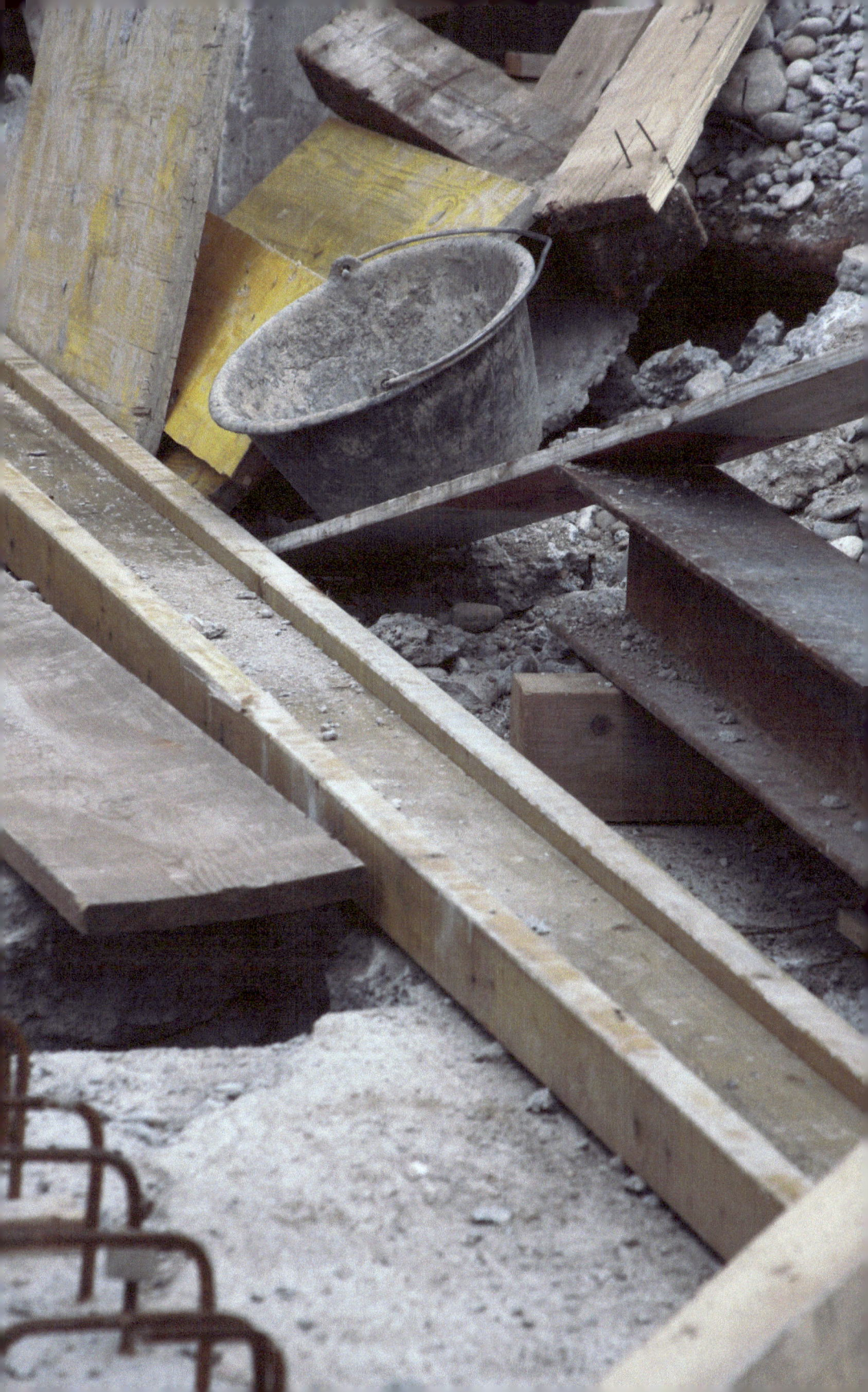

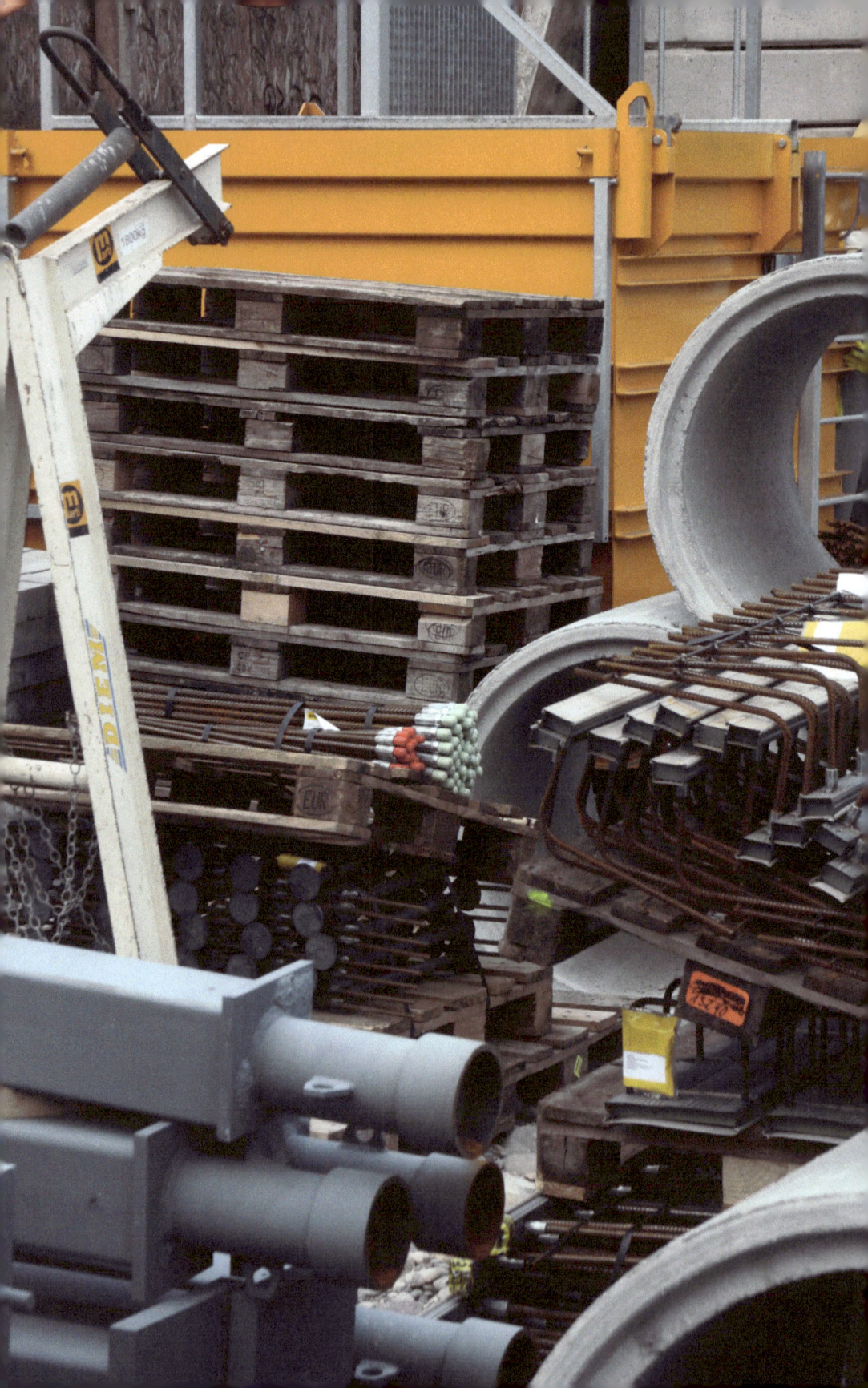

"Two minutes," Paul said.

Members of the first MediCorp team were at their usual posts, near where Jon would return. The second team was set up in the operating room. They had already staged the area so they could provide instant surgical assistance, should Jon need it.

"I never like waiting for the fog to clear," Se said. "But it'll be an agony this time. A whole day before we know for sure what he discovered. And –"

Se paused in mid-sentence and wheeled around, as they all did. The security door had just clicked, indicating that someone was entering the Decontamination Chamber and was about to enter the control site, less than two minutes before the return.

"We've got less than two minutes!" Paul said. "I don't think even J-rex has the clearance to enter the site this late."

Lat was just as surprised. "Well, somebody does. I can't think of anybody else who would show up, and especially this late."

Each time Jon had been sent forward into the future, the building and grounds had been locked down. But on his return trips? The security could not have been tighter. They had run 21 trips so far for Jon, plus a couple for Se and a few for some animals. Nobody had *ever* entered the control site any time in the two-day window around the return. A minute and a half before the return was beyond unexpected. . . .

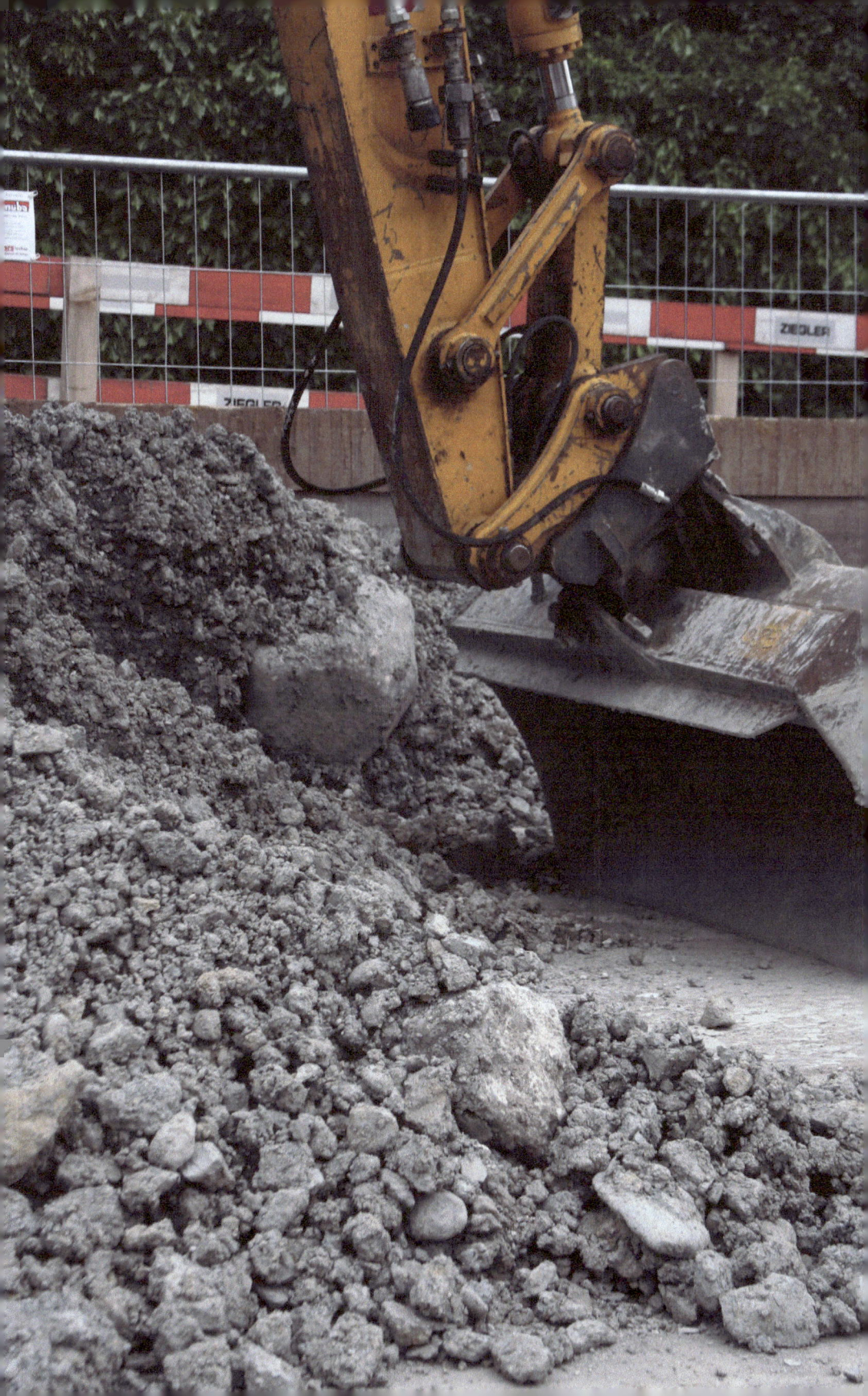

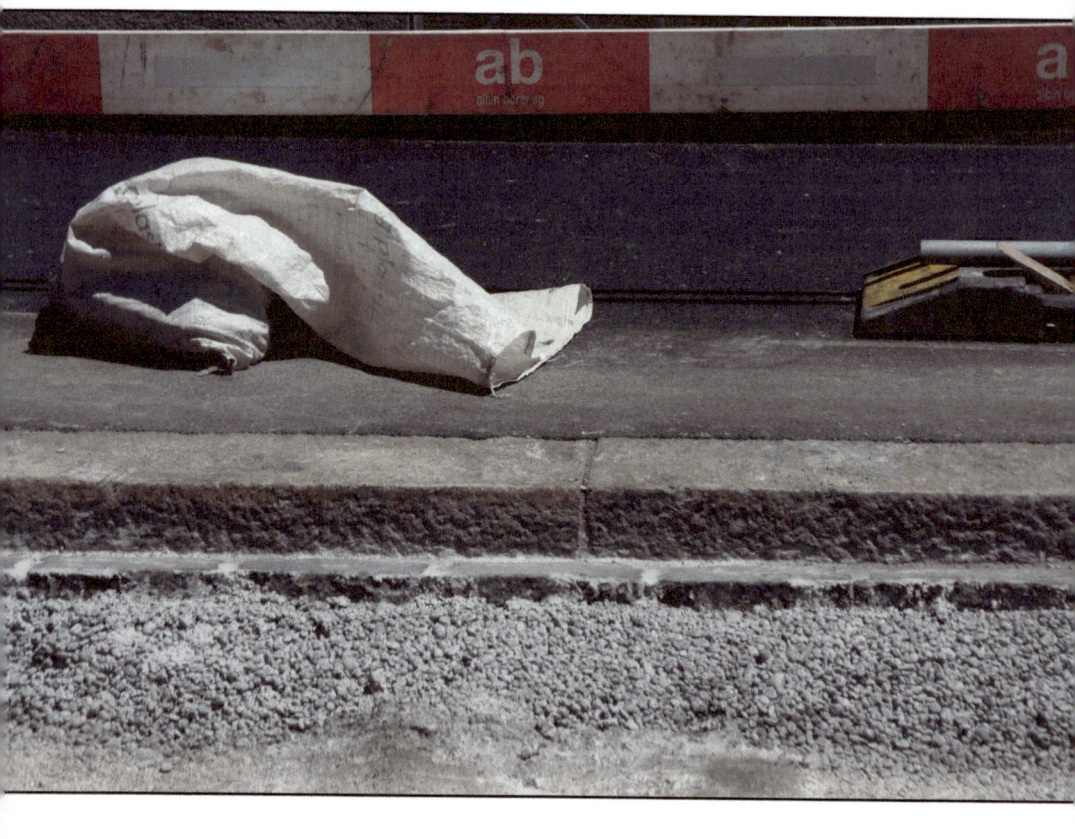

All three were prepared to see J-rex walk through the door. But none of them were ready for the eight heavily armed SecurPatrol guards who burst through the door and – ignoring them – quickly fanned out around the return site, encircling it and training their weapons on the spot where Jon would appear.

"He'll be in a fog when he comes back," Lat said. "He'll be unable to move for hours, maybe a day. You have no reason to shoot."

"You have your orders, we have ours," barked one of the men.

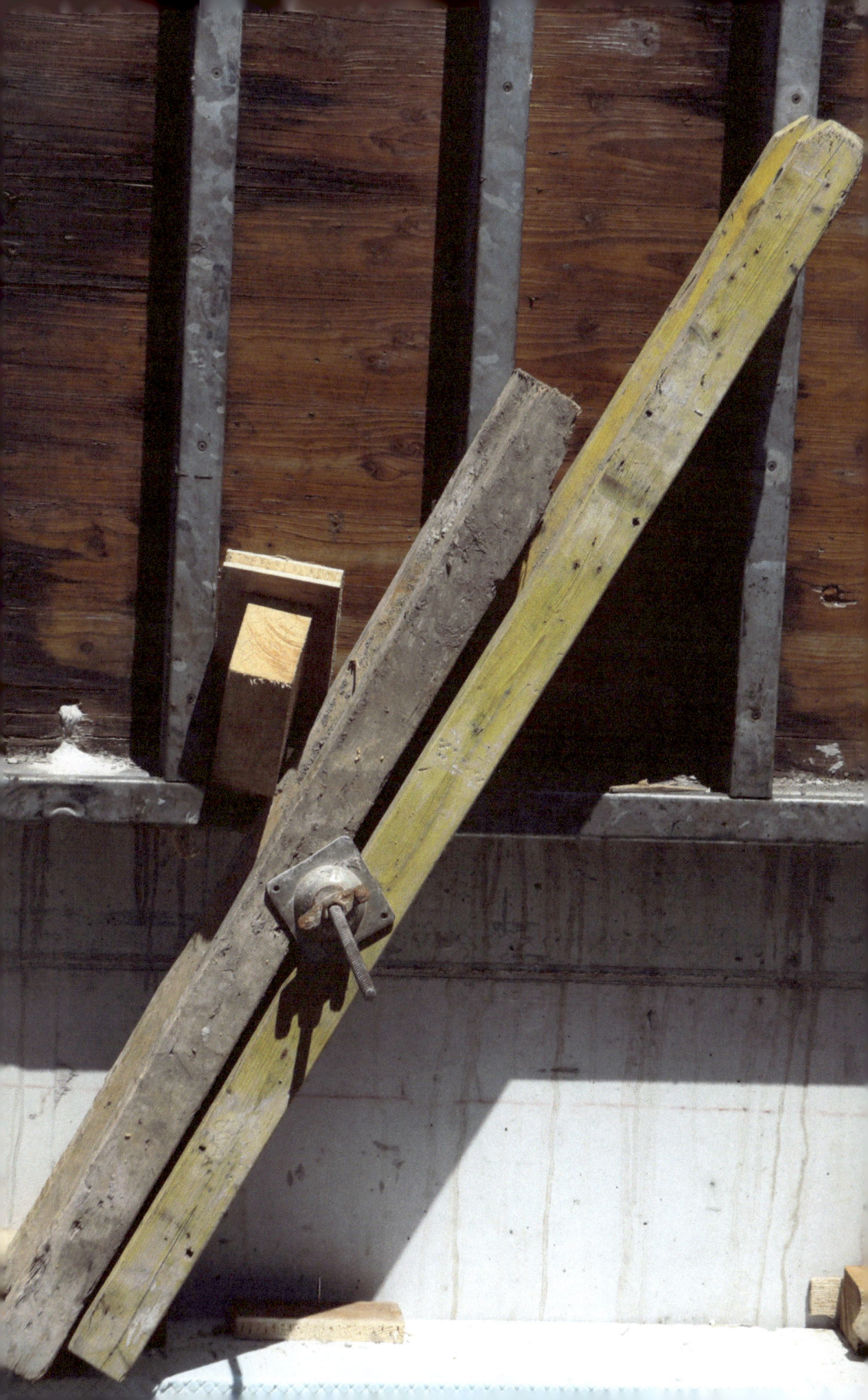

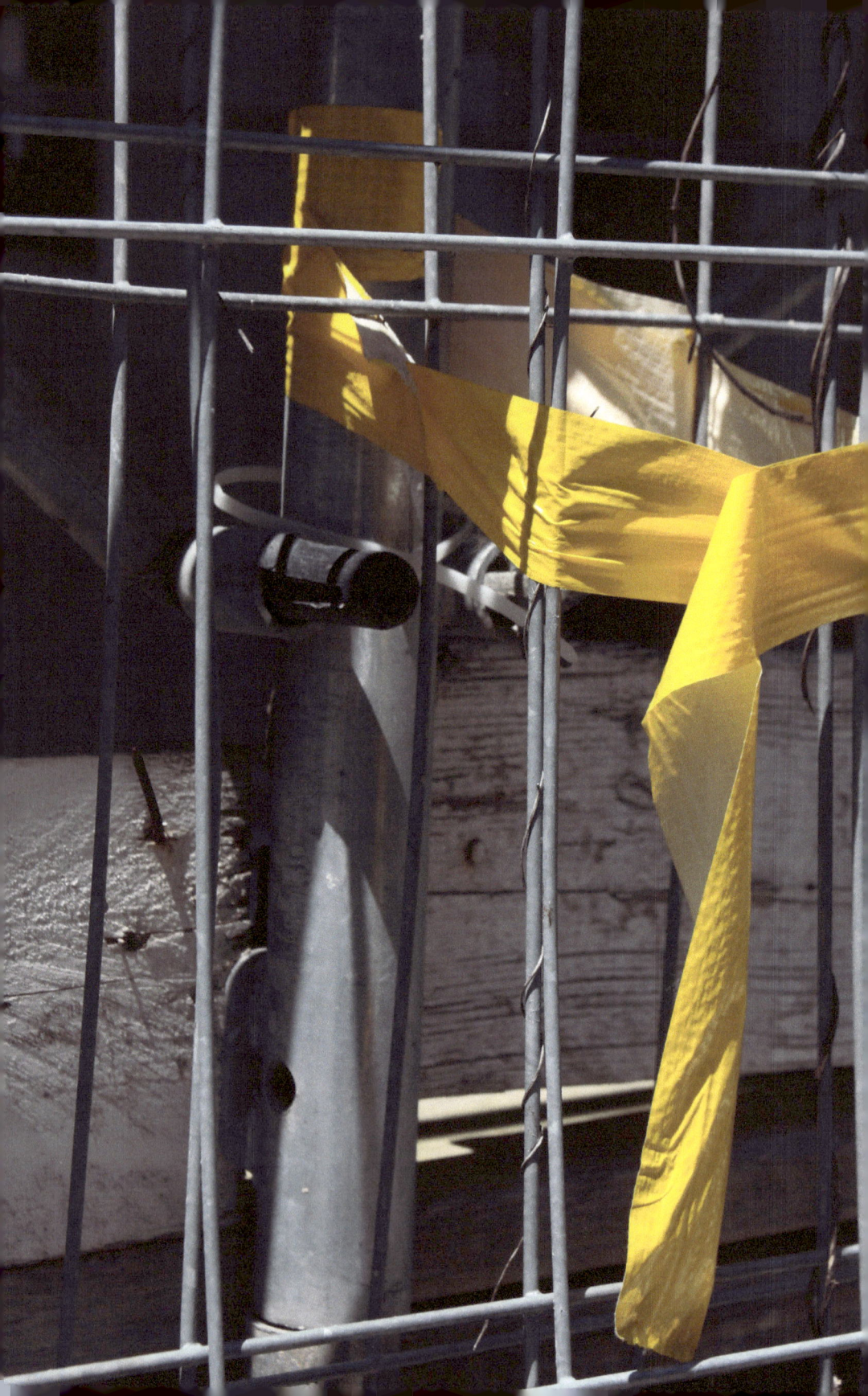

J-rex's voice burst over the InfoCom. "Paul - Se - Lat - It's alright." They stiffened. If it was really alright, why wasn't he present?

"The Corporation wants to practice this return with extra security as a drill. It's in case we ever need more security in the future," J-rex said. "They want to see what protocols need to be developed. Don't let it spook you. It's just a practice in case we have an emergency sometime in the future."

"Sixty seconds," Paul said.

Lat and Se reflexively returned to their posts. None of the three said any more. They had plenty to monitor on their controls. But they all knew each other well enough that they could read each other's expressions.

So, for that matter, could J-rex, watching from the remote control tower. "Relax," he said again. "It's alright." But they knew J-rex never did anything accidentally. And that meant it was probably not alright.

The three were fast at computing. J-rex had inadvertently revealed he was at the remote control tower. The one that, when it was built a year prior, he had said would never be used. "Just a precaution. For emergencies."

And now he was using it. He hadn't just been gone the past two days. He'd been silently watching the operation on 20-foot monitors from the remote.

Lat had seen the monitors a couple weeks before the tower was completed. But even Lat's security clearance wasn't high enough to get into the tower once it was finished.

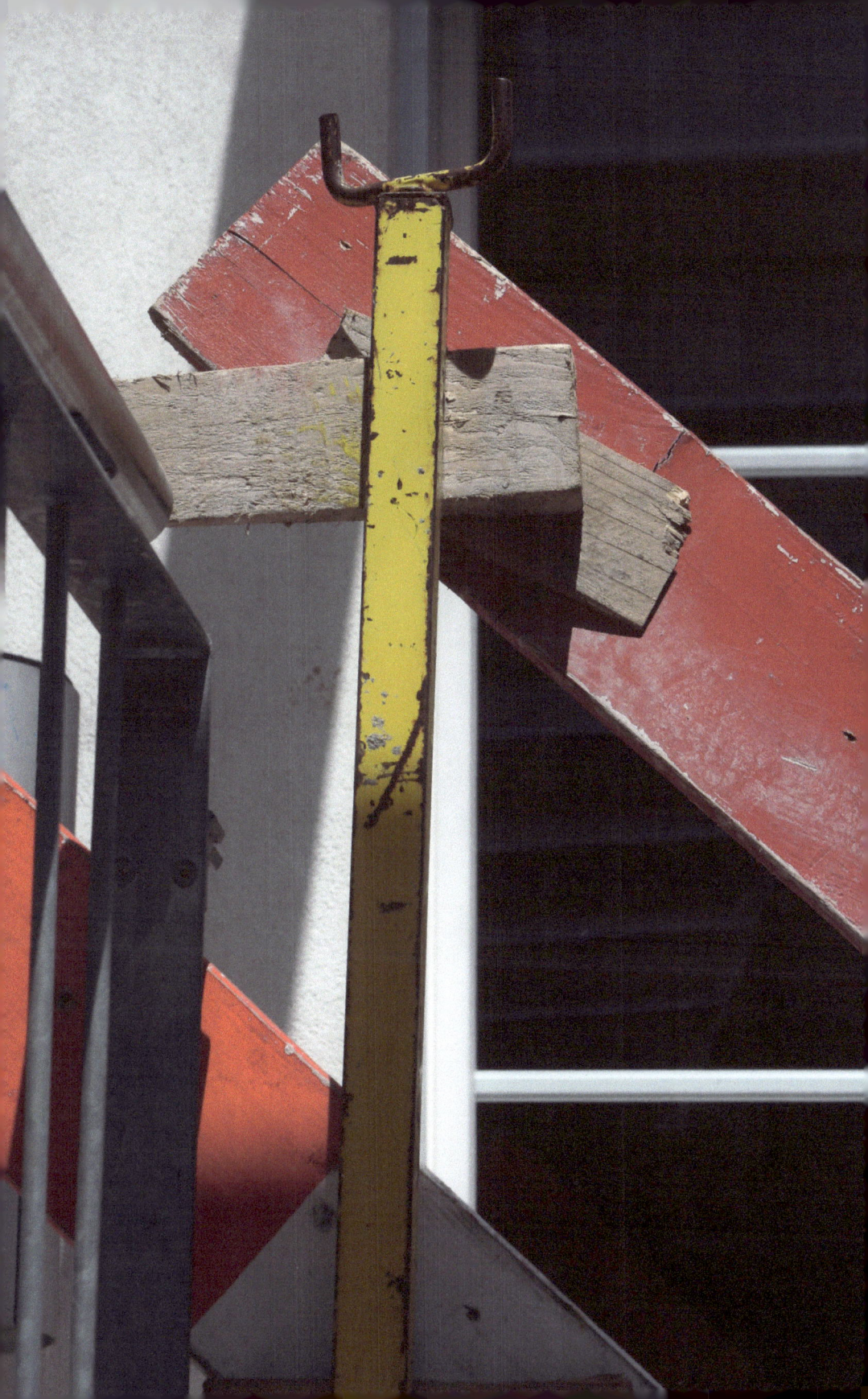

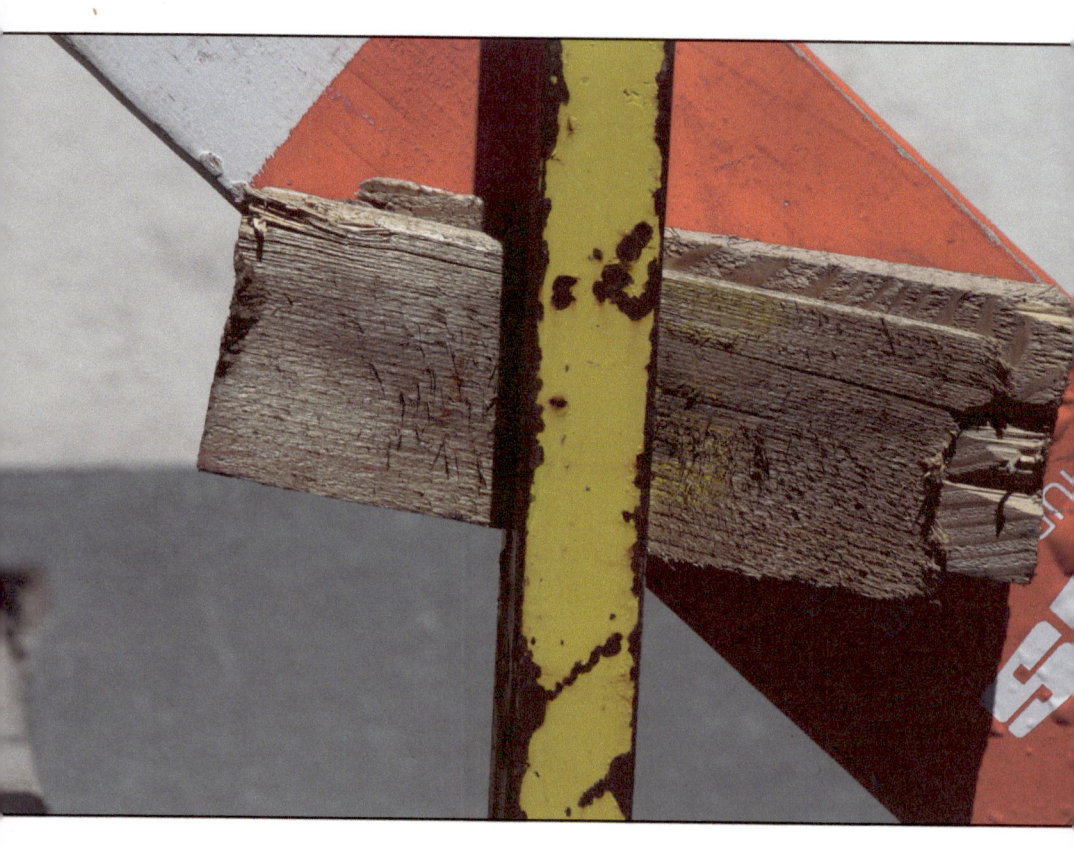

With J-rex's location now known and the eight armed SecurPatrols in the room, the three were hyper-vigilant. As a result, all three noticed it at the same time, a split second before the shift.

And it was worse than they expected.

Jon's body mass and position were wrong.

And then the timeshift struck and Jon materialized – or what should have been Jon.

The eight guards had their weapons trained on where the heart should have been of an upright man. But what came back from the future wasn't upright. And it wasn't a man.

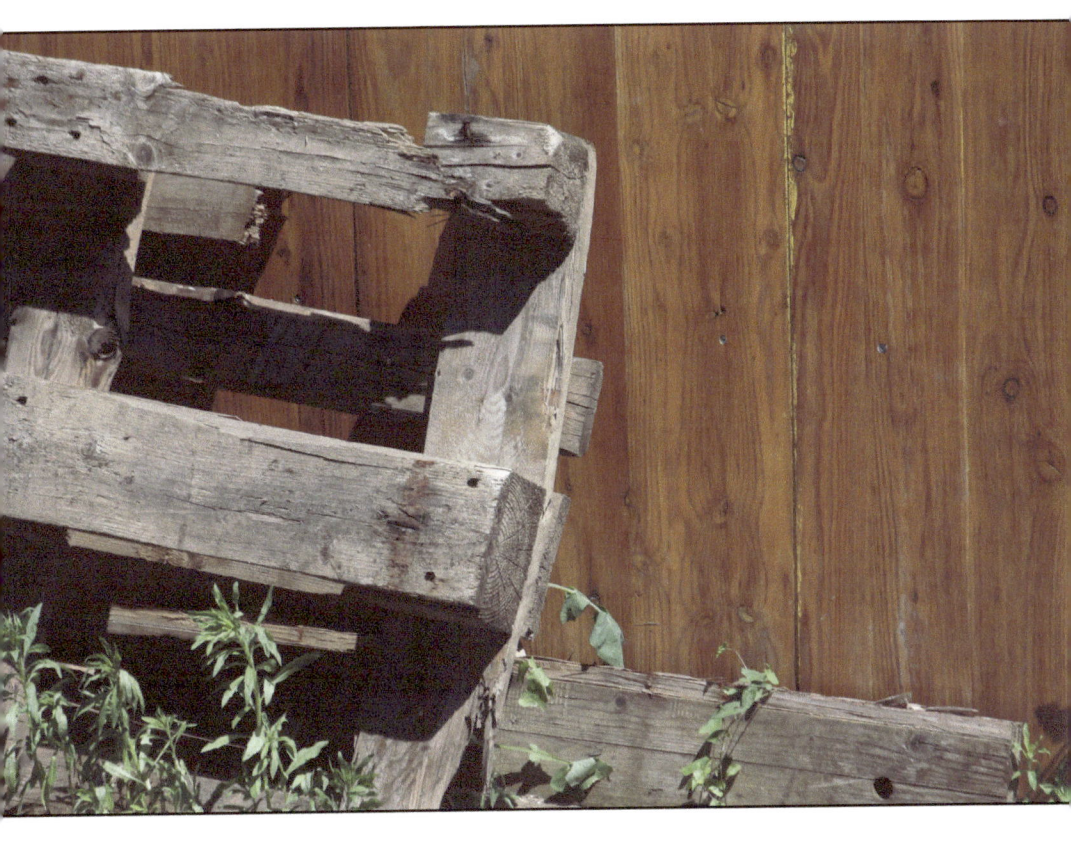

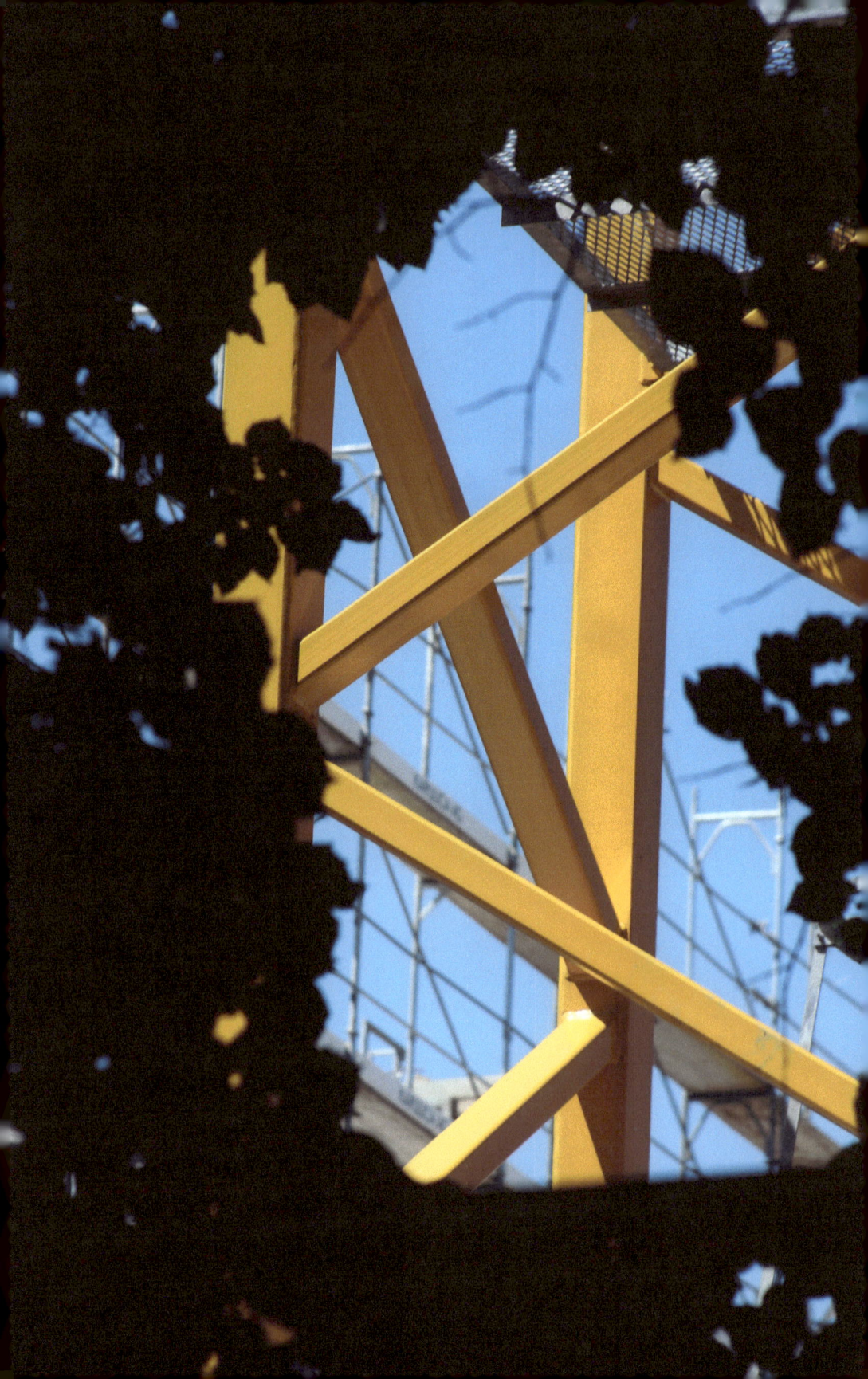

Se gasped. He quickly checked the coordinates and saw he had done everything right. He next checked Paul and Lat's work. Everything was okay. Except the result.

On the floor of the return site, instead of Jon, lay a motionless alligator.

"Careful," said Lat. "They move fast, when they want to. And they have no brain to speak of, so they might not arrive in a fog."

But even as he spoke, they could see that the animal wasn't going to be moving. One of its legs was decomposed. The creature had been dead for some time.

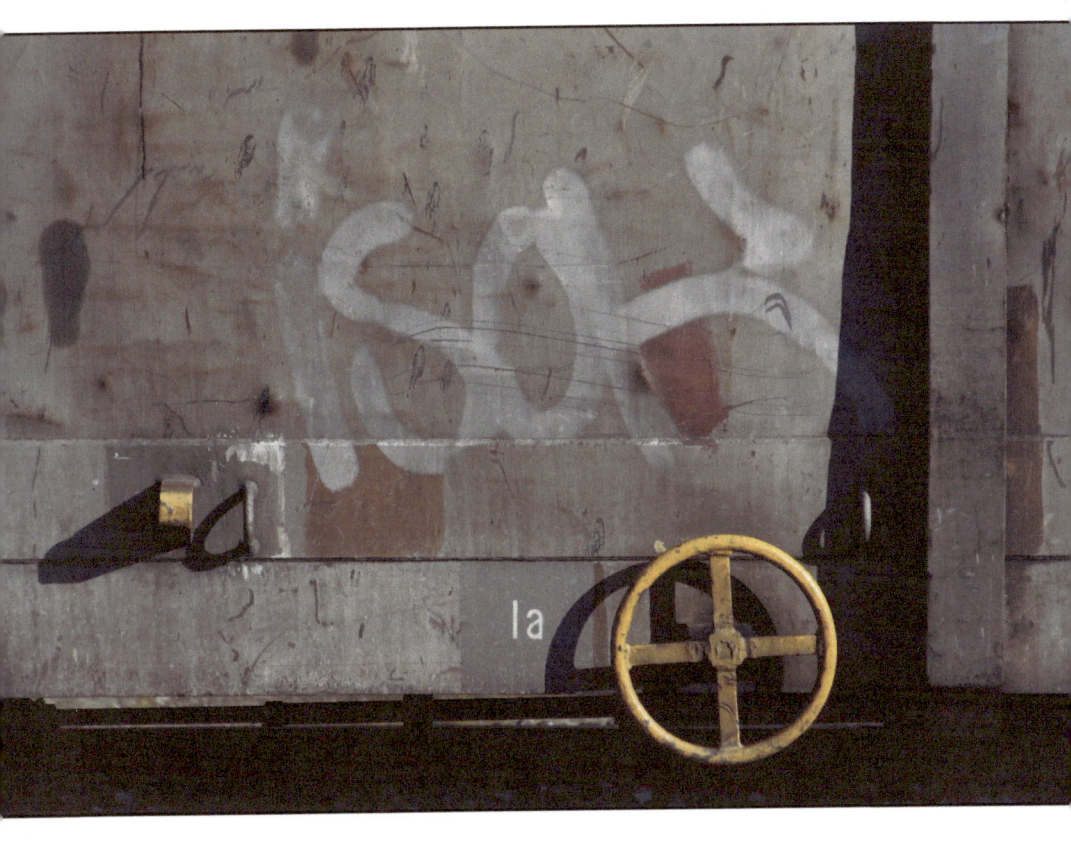

la

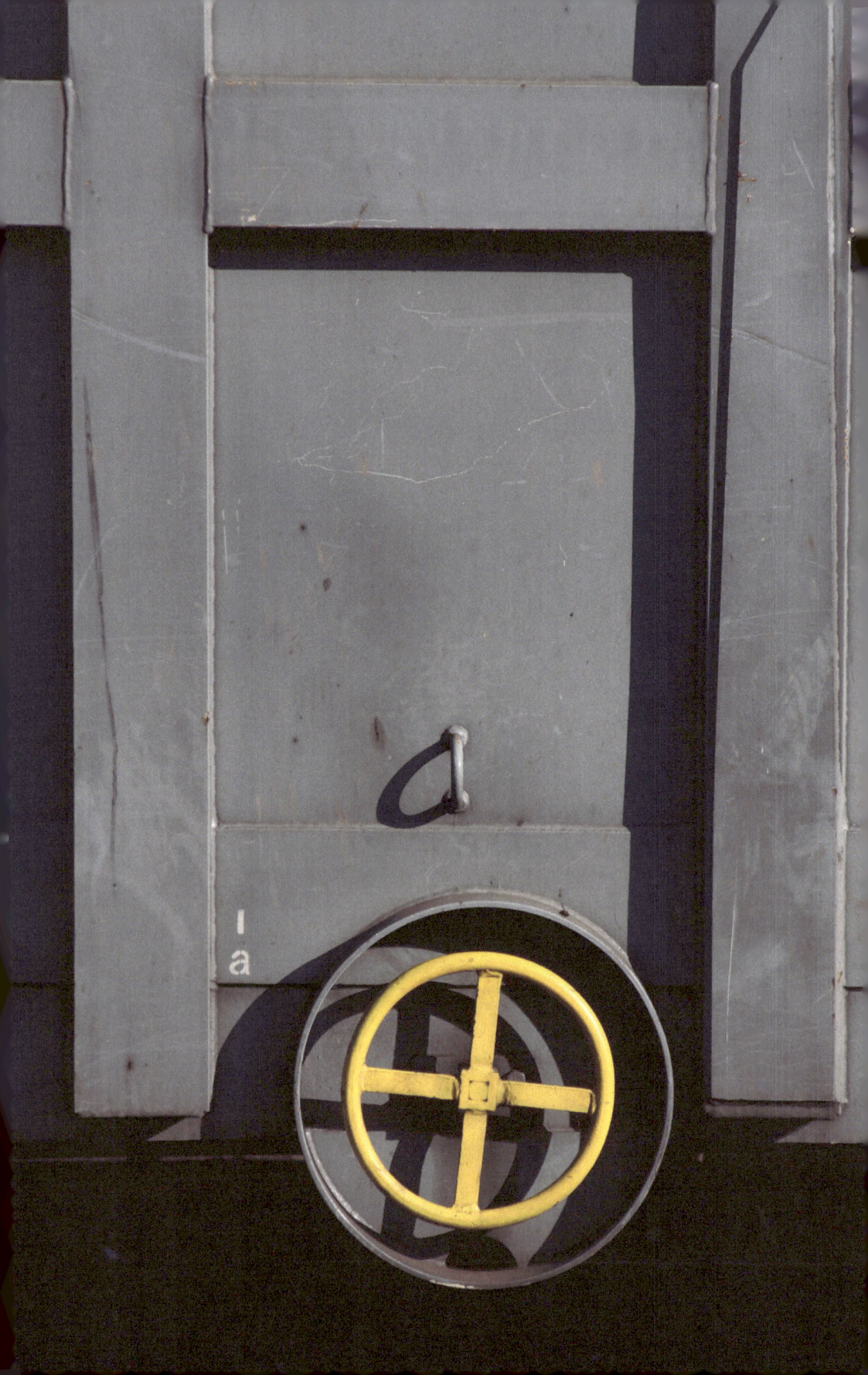

"Where's Jon?" Se shouted. He was looking at all the monitors. "The scans don't show that he was anywhere inside the perimeter."

"He's stuck *outside* the perimeter?" Paul had monitored the hyptrolysis session for J-rex and everything had gone well. Jon had been programmed to go outside the perimeter, thinking it was his own idea. But he was supposed to make it back.

Paul had known it was a possibility that Jon wouldn't return; he had even talked about it. But he hadn't thought it would happen. How could Jon not have made it back?

J-rex was on the InfoCom. "How did that gator get picked up? Did it just crawl onto the coordinates?"

Se had been looking at it. "I don't think it crawled there. Look at the back leg. It hasn't been moving on its own for some time."

J-rex wasn't sure one bad leg would slow down a gator. But it did *look* dead.

"Right. MediCorp Team One: Check out the gator. Everyone else, stay at your positions until we sort this out."

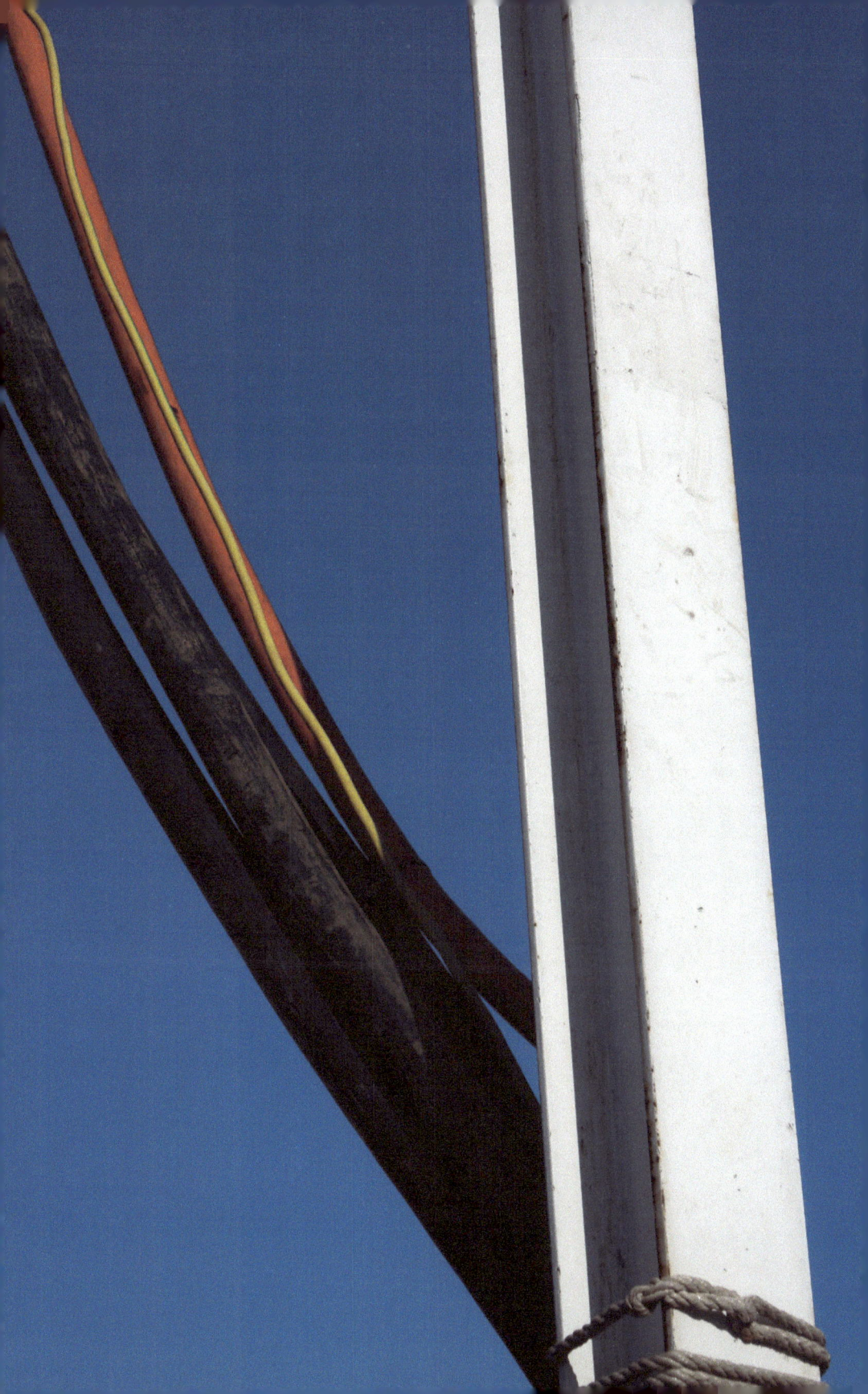

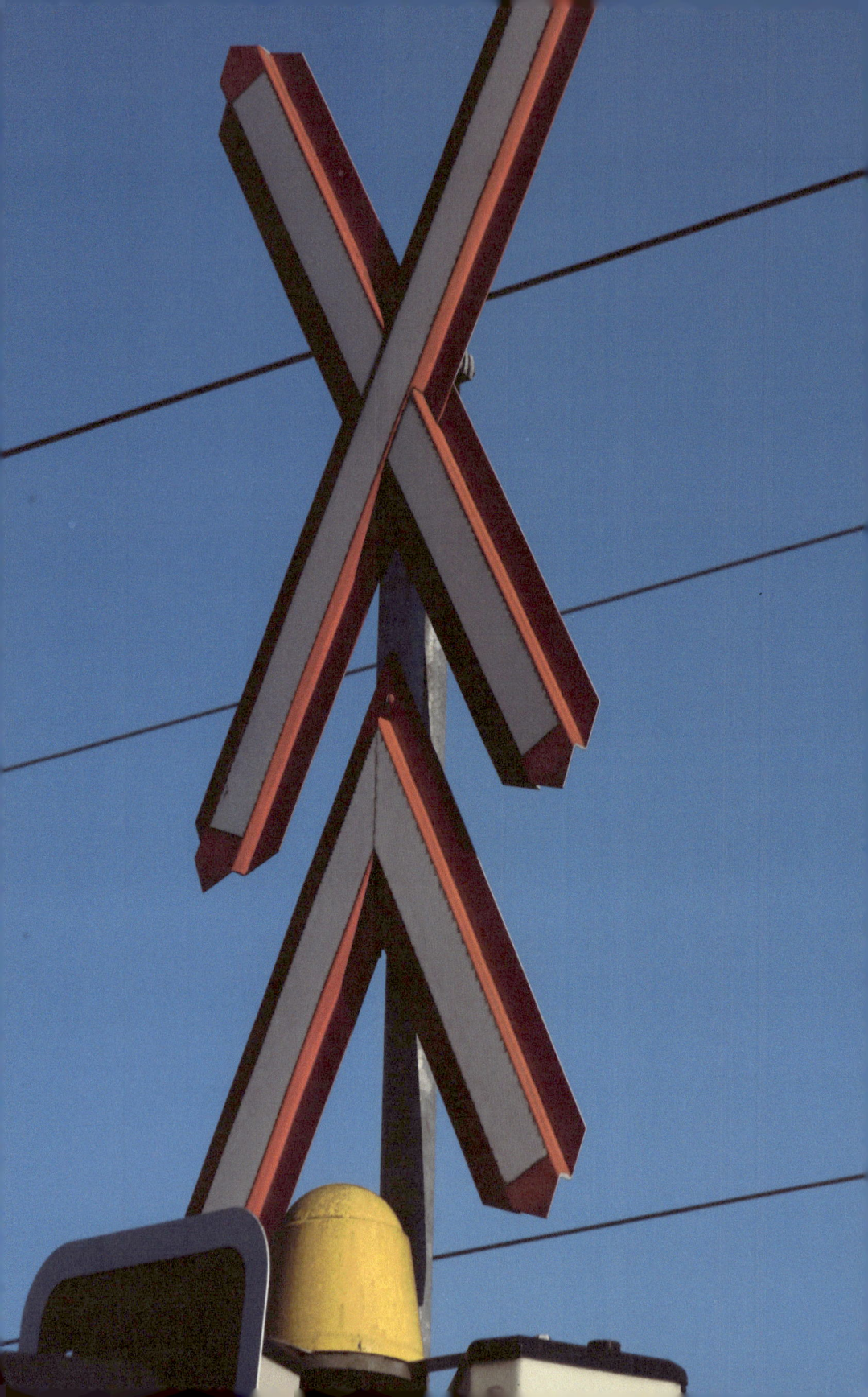

The team did a quick scan and found what Se had suspected: the gator had been dead for some time. Inside it was a mess. Some tissues were intact, but the brain, heart and liver were liquefied. They found nothing else of note in their exam.

* * *

The site remained in lockdown an extra three days, but at the end of that time they were no closer to knowing for sure what had happened. By then they were irritated, tired, and bored. They had poured over the data dozens of times, maybe even hundreds of times, and had found nothing new.

Even the gator's surgical exam by MediCorp Team Two had found nothing different from what the initial scans by Team One had revealed.

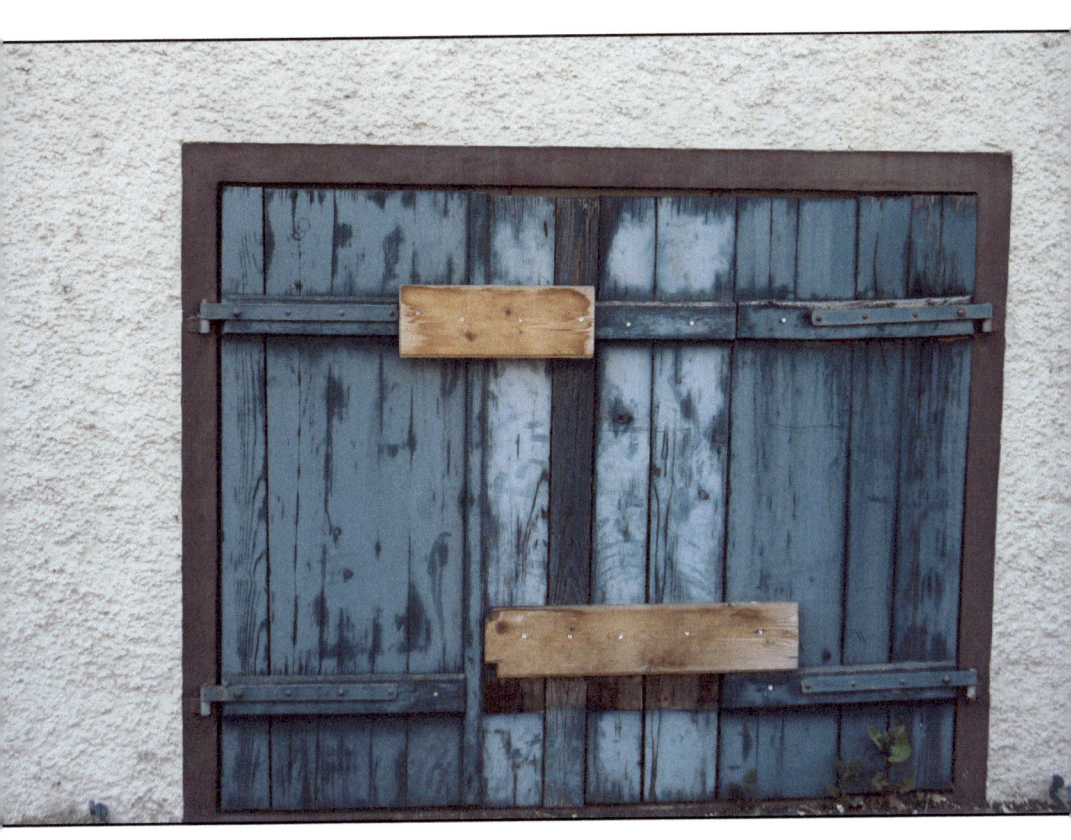

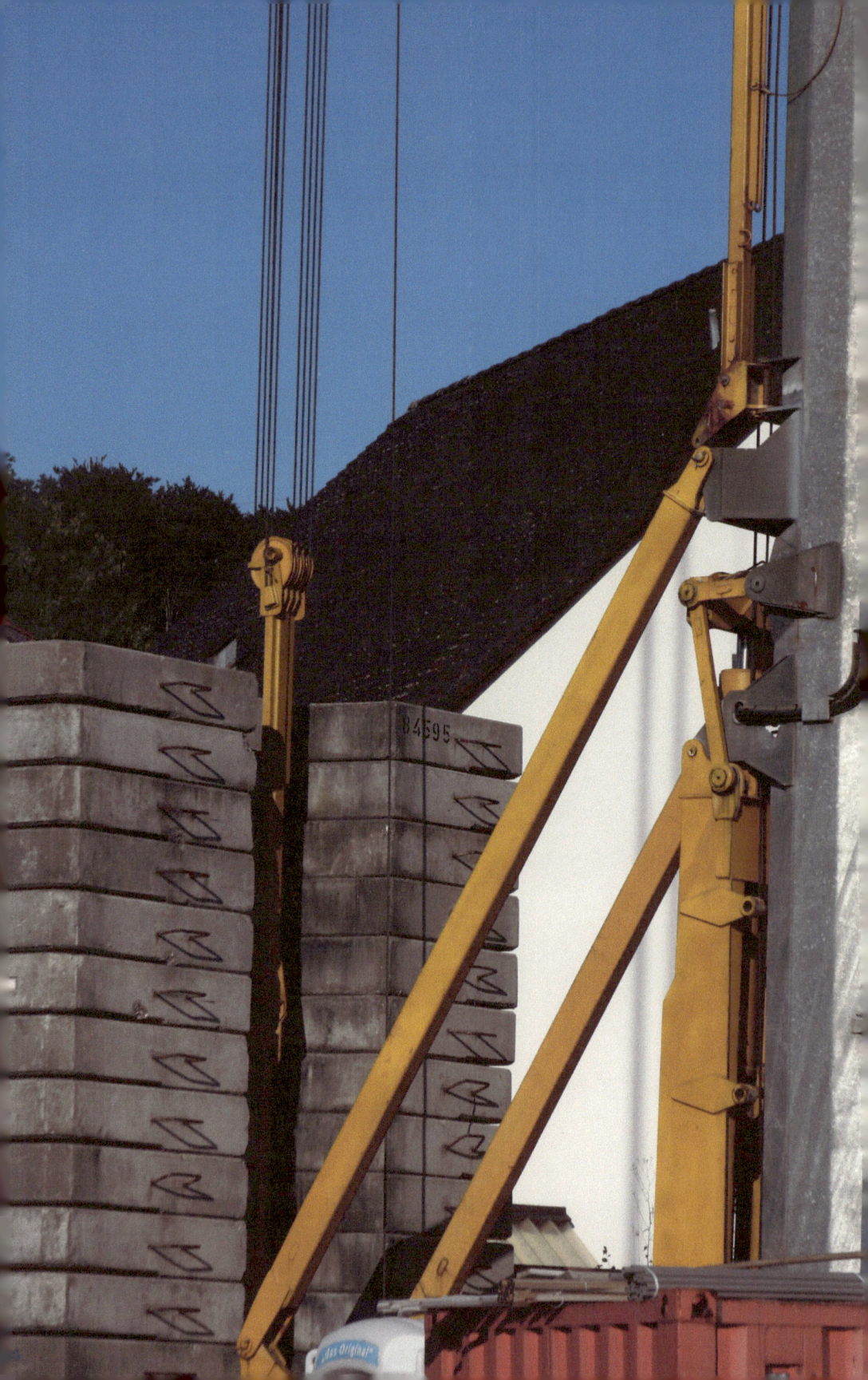

J-rex was running things from the remote. He said he wouldn't be released from the remote for another month since the Corporation wanted a full test of the remote's equipment to make sure it was built to spec. But he was back in charge, if not visibly present.

Se was making preparations for a trip to discover what had happened in the future and – if possible – to rescue Jon. But his mission wouldn't be ready for three more days. Everyone was cleared to go home for a short break.

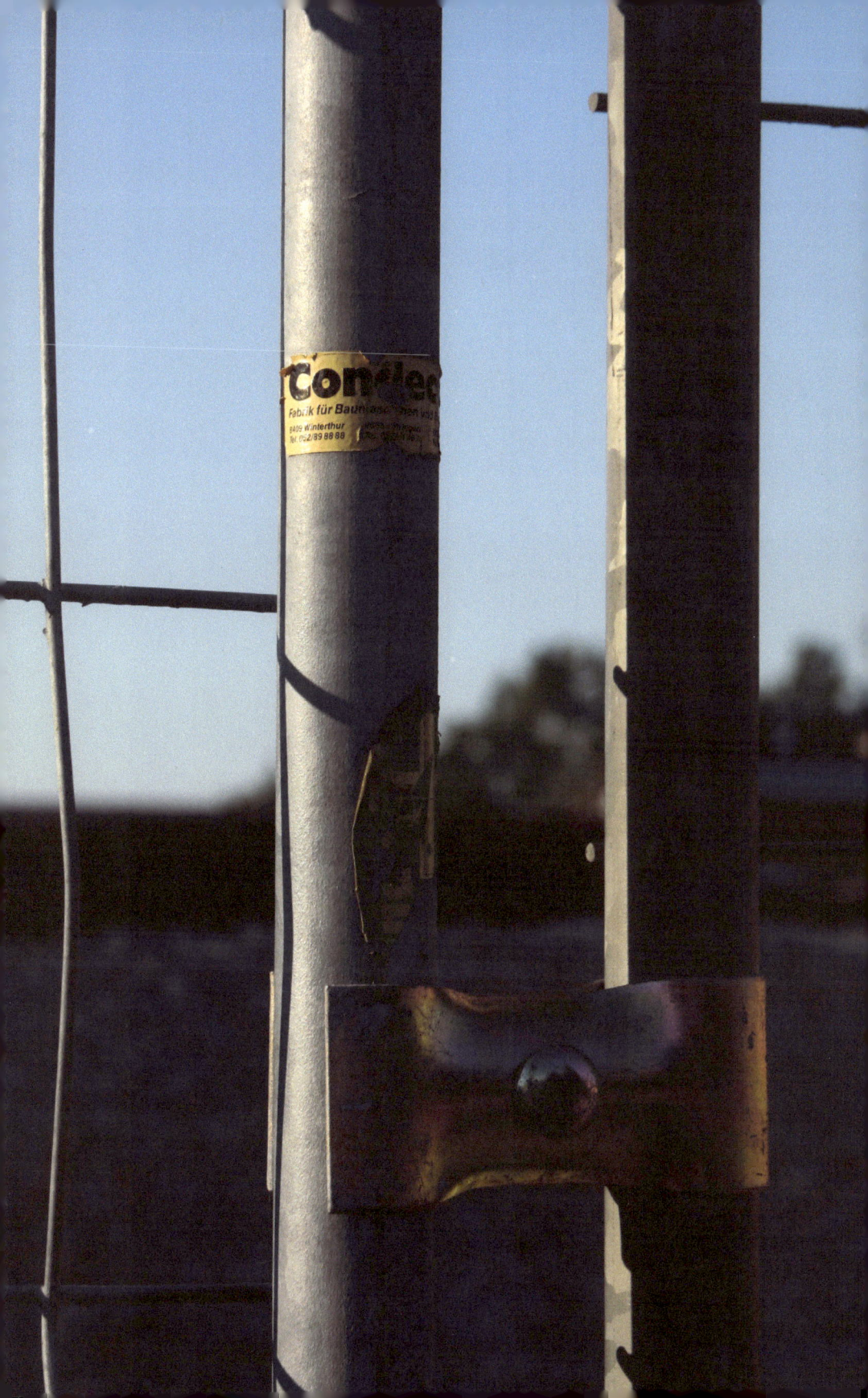

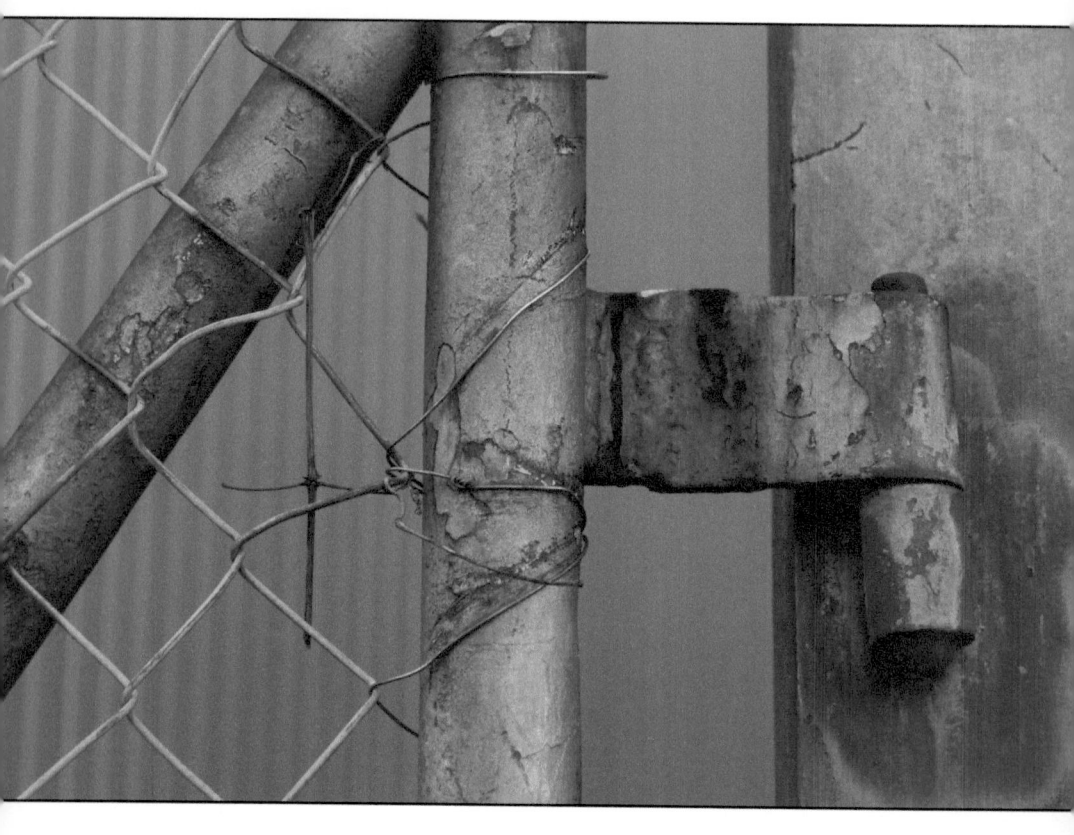

Lat was uneasy. Something (besides the gator) still wasn't right. But he couldn't identify it.

For the past three days they had been focused on the gator and on Jon's disappearance. They had been working with thirteen extra team members crammed into the space and were still getting used to J-rex being at the remote. In all that confusion, it was not surprising that Lat missed the one tiny piece of medical data that he needed to notice.

As the MediCorp teams left the site, Team Two checked out with a ten gram variance on their weight. It was so slight, and they had all been there so many extra days, it could have been anything.

But it was not just anything. It was a present from Jon and from the future, now inside one of the five members of Team Two, the reason the alligator's brain, heart and liver had been mush.

The liver of one of the members of Team Two was already mostly liquefied, and her brain was going to be next.

Lat hit the clearance for everyone to pass through the Decontamination Chamber. Then he left with them.

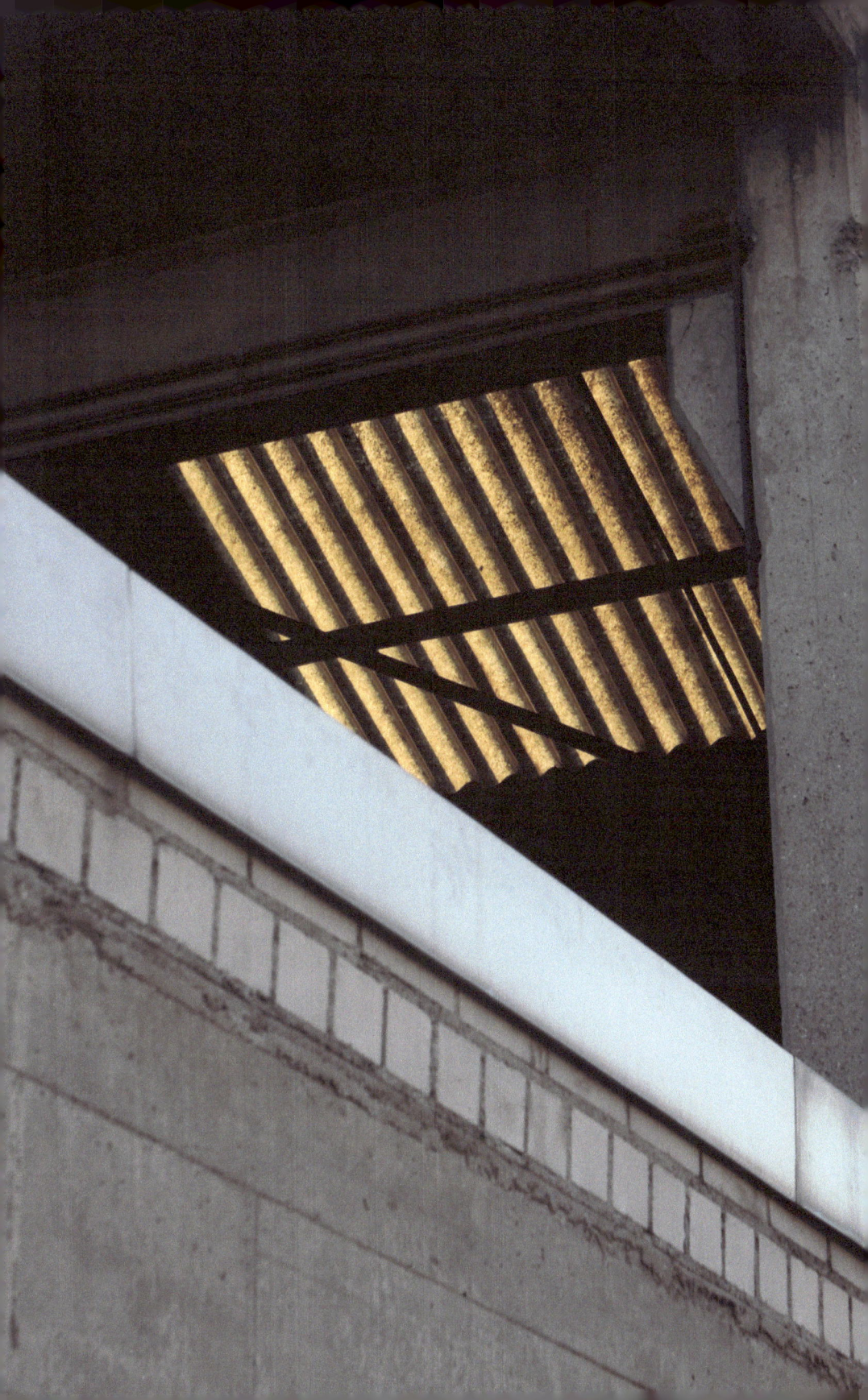

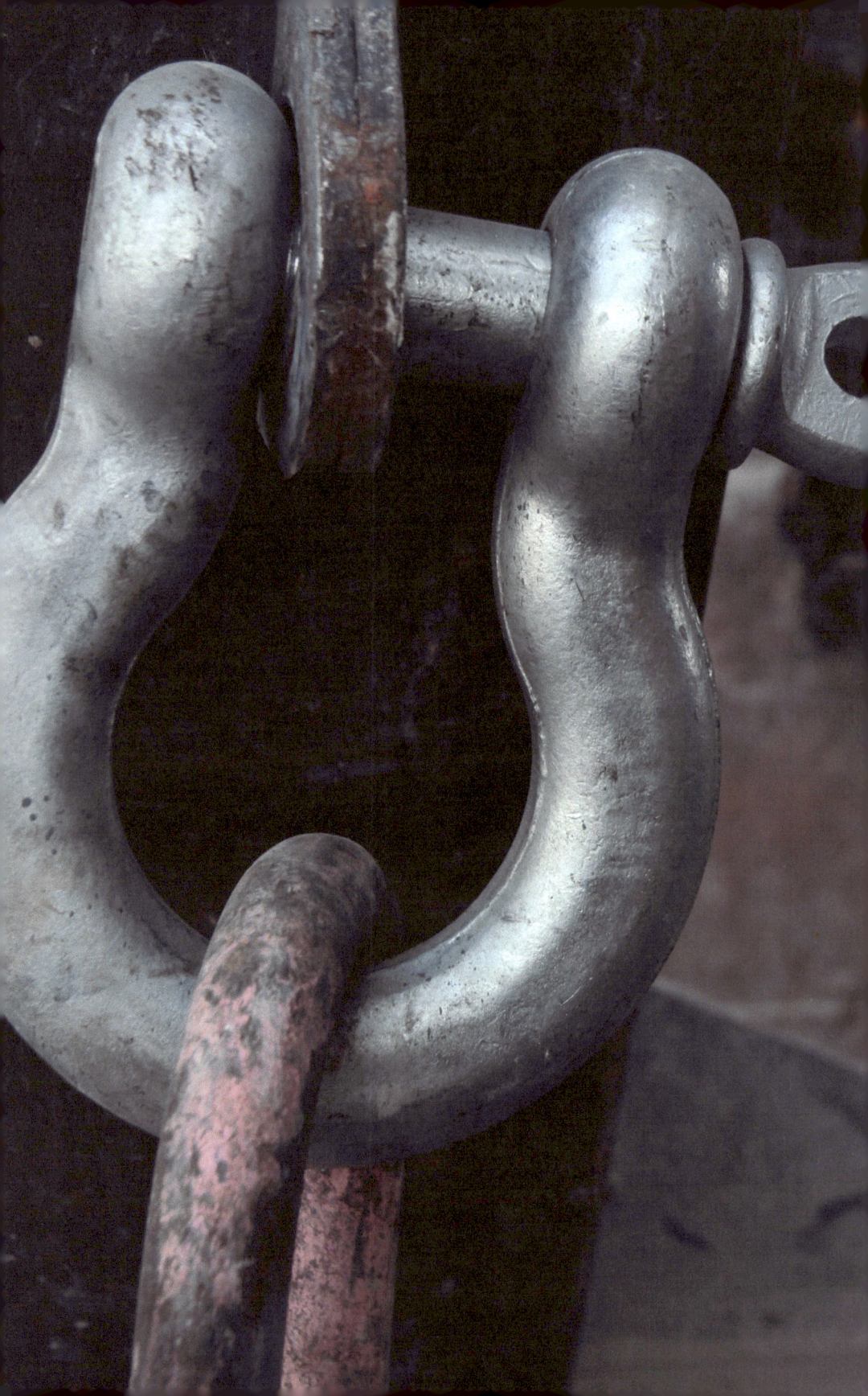

J-rex watched another minute on the monitor from the remote tower. Then he turned his back on the screen and headed out to take a break.

Five minutes after everyone had cleared the room, the carcass of the dead alligator began to move.

~~

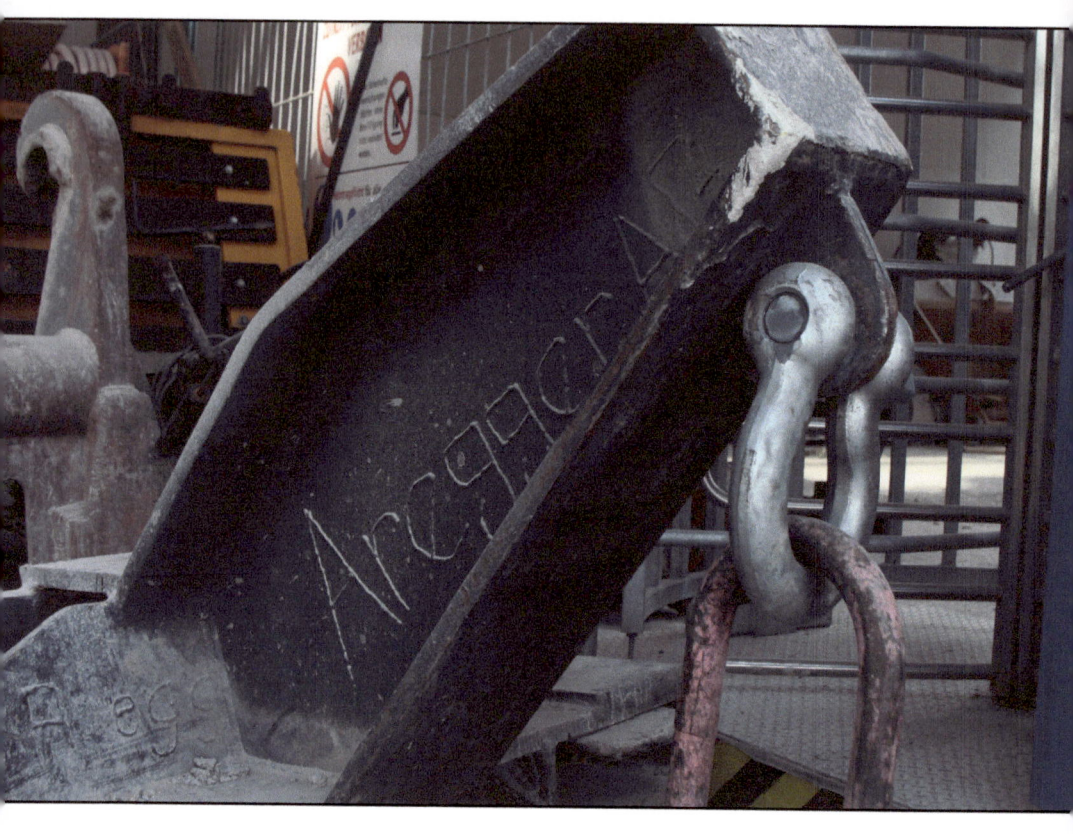

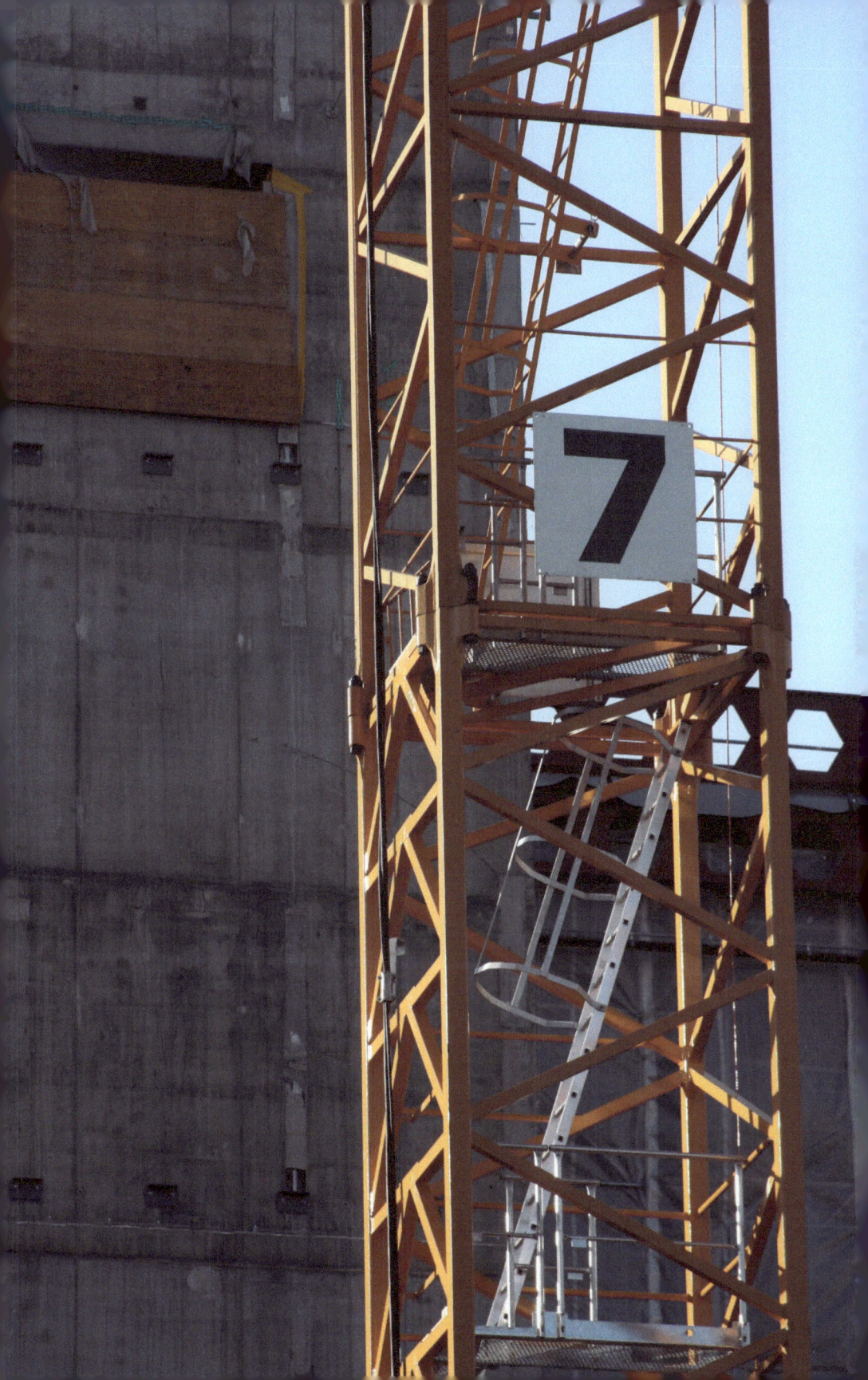

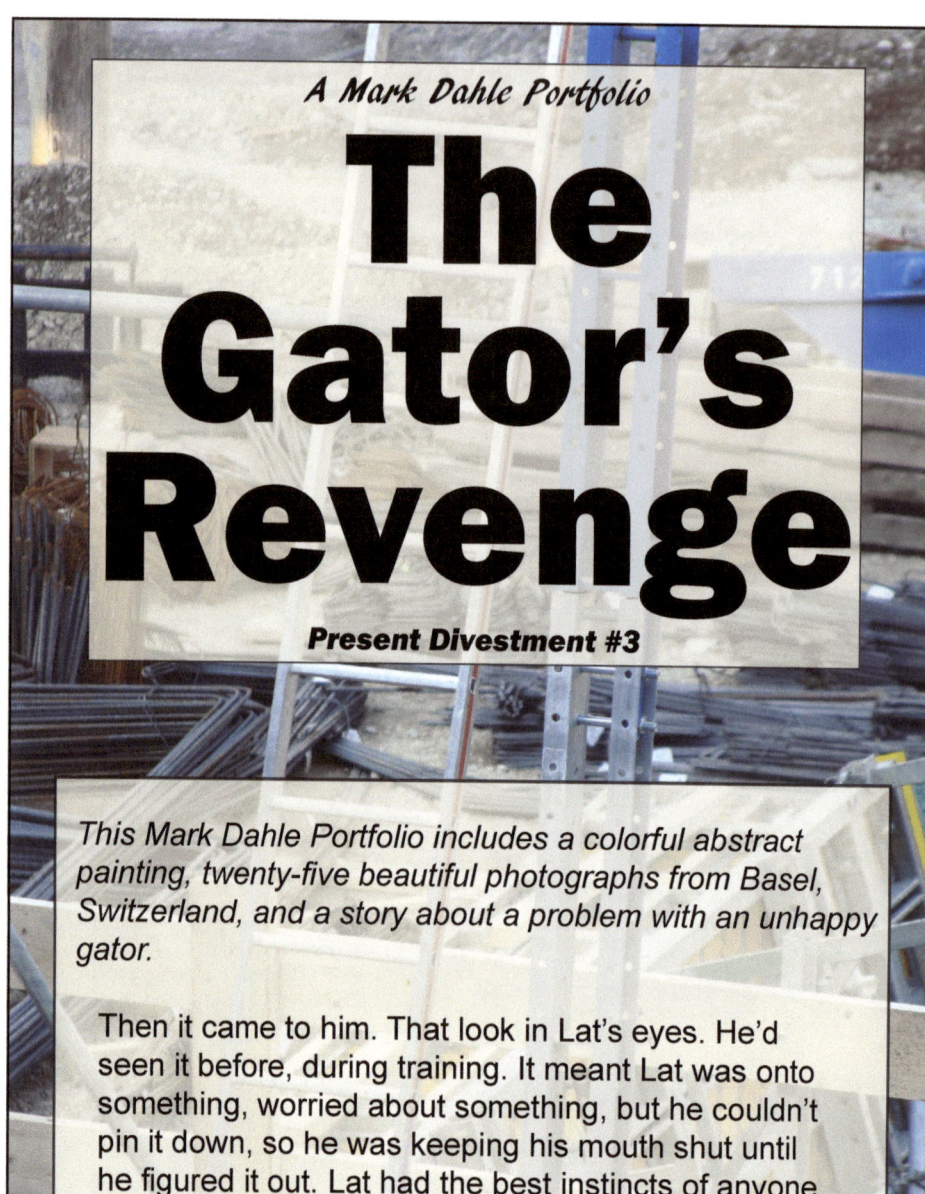

A Mark Dahle Portfolio

The Gator's Revenge

Present Divestment #3

This Mark Dahle Portfolio includes a colorful abstract painting, twenty-five beautiful photographs from Basel, Switzerland, and a story about a problem with an unhappy gator.

Then it came to him. That look in Lat's eyes. He'd seen it before, during training. It meant Lat was onto something, worried about something, but he couldn't pin it down, so he was keeping his mouth shut until he figured it out. Lat had the best instincts of anyone J-rex knew. Why was Lat worried when he was about to take his first break in five days?

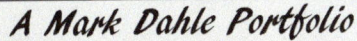

A Mark Dahle Portfolio

Lat's Collapse

Present Divestment #4

This Mark Dahle Portfolio includes a colorful abstract painting, twenty-five beautiful photographs from Basel, Switzerland, and a story about some problems with time travel.

Fifteen minutes before, the room had been sterile and clean. Now there was broken glass everywhere, smashed equipment, small fires, electric sparks showering from slashed wires, smoke, and, he finally saw, movement – a gator racing the length of the room straight towards Lat, moving as fast as it could go.

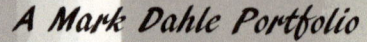

A Mark Dahle Portfolio

Derrack's Folly

Present Divestment #5

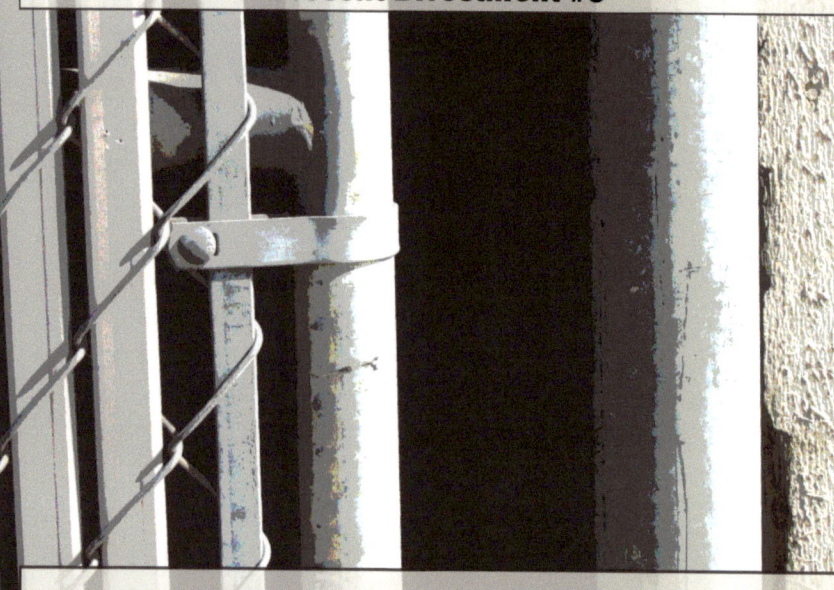

This Mark Dahle Portfolio includes a colorful abstract painting, twenty-six slightly altered photographs, and a story about a mom trying to stay calm in an emergency.

Lisa smiled and relaxed. In five minutes she'd be at the school picking up her kids. This was going to be easy.

www.ingramcontent.com/pod-product-compliance
Lightning Source LLC
Chambersburg PA
CBHW040901180526
45159CB00001B/487